WEE SHOPS

DOUGLAS CORRANCE

RICHARD DREW PUBLISHING

GLASGOW

DOUGLAS CORRANCE

AFTER ELEVEN YEARS AS PHOTOGRAPHER
WITH THE SCOTTISH TOURIST BOARD,
DOUGLAS CORRANCE SET UP ON HIS OWN
IN 1985 AS A FREELANCE PHOTOGRAPHER,
SPECIALIZING IN TOURISM AND TRAVEL.
HE IS INTERNATIONALLY REGARDED FOR
WORK OF THE HIGHEST QUALITY.

HE FEELS STRONGLY THAT SMALL SHOPS
AND SUB-POST OFFICES HAVE AN
IMPORTANT ROLE TO PLAY IN THE
COMMUNITY, WHETHER SITUATED IN THE
CITY OR THE COUNTRYSIDE AND ARE WELL
WORTH PRESERVING AGAINST THE RISING
TIDE OF UNIFORMITY AND
SUPERMARKETS.

© DOUGLAS CORRANCE 1988

FIRST PUBLISHED 1988
BY RICHARD DREW PUBLISHING LIMITED
6 CLAIRMONT GARDENS
GLASGOW G3 7LW, SCOTLAND

ISBN 0 86267 229 5

DESIGNED BY JAMES W. MURRAY

REPRODUCTION BY SWAINS, EDINBURGH
MADE AND PRINTED IN GREAT BRITAIN
BY THE EAGLE PRESS PLC, GLASGOW

EDINBURGH

SOUTH QUEENSFERRY, NEAR EDINBURGH

NEWPORT ON TAY, FIFE

BALLATER, DEESIDE

GLASGOW

ABERDEEN

AYR

DUNDEE

THE ARCADE, INVERNESS

GLASGOW

GLASGOW

GLASGOW

EDINBURGH

GLASGOW

GLASGOW

ROTHESAY, ISLE OF BUTE

GOLSPIE, SUTHERLAND

PERTH

EDINBURGH

EDINBURGH

DUNFERMLINE, FIFE

GLASGOW

EDINBURGH

GLASGOW

GLASGOW

GLASGOW

GLASGOW

LARGS, CLYDE COAST

GRETNA GREEN, ANNANDALE AND ESKDALE

GLASGOW